NEVER BE
HURT AGAIN

GREGORY DICKOW

How to Never Be Hurt Again
©2003 by Gregory Dickow Ministries.

Unless otherwise noted, all Scripture quotations in this
volume are from the *King James Version* of the Bible.

Scripture quotations marked (NASB) are taken from
the New American Standard Bible®
Copyright © 1960, 1962, 1963, 1968, 1971, 1972,
1973, 1975, 1977, 1995 by The Lockman Foundation
Used by permission. (www.Lockman.org)

Printed in the United States of America

For information, please write
Gregory Dickow Ministries,
P.O. Box 7000
Chicago, IL 60680

or visit us online at www.changinglives.org.

Table of Contents

WE HAVE ALL BEEN HURT

Chapter One

"Sticks and stones can break my bones, but names will never hurt me." Whoever used to say that when we were kids was the one who was usually hurt! It's just not true. Names hurt us. Words hurt us. Being lied about hurts us. Being misunderstood can be hurtful as well.

Proverbs 12:18 says, *"There is one who speaks like the piercings of a sword..."*

One of the most difficult things people deal with is being hurt. Hurt feelings rob us of so many of God's blessings.

Before you can really move on in your life, you have to take the hurt out. You can't build upon a foundation of hurt. It will distort your decisions and your view of everything else in your life. It will make you bitter toward others and prevent you from going forward.

The Way Out. I am going to share with you how to never be hurt again for the rest of your life. Somebody said, "You don't know what I am going through. I came from a dysfunctional family." We all came from a dysfunctional family. We all have our gripes. We all have had reason to feel like we got the wrong end of the deal.

Maybe you've been hurt in a business situation. Maybe you've been hurt in a marriage or you've been through a divorce.

Maybe you've been hurt through child abuse. Maybe you've been hurt through something you are continually referring to as, the reason you are the way you are.

We must stop finding our point of reference in our past pain. Our point of reference has to be the day Jesus came into our life and turned our life around and gave us a new beginning. My point of reference is not my past pain. In fact, it's not my past at all. I didn't get born again until I was seventeen years old. So up until that time—from the time I was born till the time I was born again—as far as I'm concerned, that wasn't even me!

The Bible says, *"If any man is in Christ, he's a new creature. The old things are passed away and all things have become new"* (2 Corinthians 5:17).

Why do we look into all of the problems of our past? What good is it going to do? Some counselors will sit down with a troubled person and tell them, "We need to go back to when you were two years old. We need to go back to when your brother stole your rattle. That seems to be where everything began to turn downward for you, and I believe I can help you from there."

No! We must dismiss what people have done to us. It doesn't matter. What matters is how we respond.

We've got to get to a place in our life where we can never be hurt and I believe the Bible tells us we can have that, beginning today!

Why We Need the Victory. We have all been around people who are hurt or offended, and they are not fun to be around. Are they?

1. Hurt people are unpleasant to be around. They talk about their past. They expect you to read their mind. They carry their emotions on their sleeve to get you to ask them about it, so they can tell you about it. And they think, "The doctor said if I talk about it, then it will help me." Well have you been helped, yet? You've been talking about it for the last ten years, and it still hasn't helped!

2. Hurt leads to anger and is sometimes turned inward producing depression. When we feel hurt, we get angry or begin to feel sorry for ourselves. We lose initiative to fight off negative feelings. They weigh us down and produce depression and stress. Stress is one of the leading causes of premature death. We need to give attention to both our emotional and physical health. But be aware that unhealthy emotions can destroy us from the inside.

3. Hurt people make bad decisions.

When we have been hurt, we tend to make decisions that protect our feelings instead of our future.

We must stop making decisions that protect our feelings, and start making decisions that protect our future. The decision that I make today is going to affect my future, and therefore I can't make a decision based on my pain or my past.

You can get to a point where no matter what somebody does to you, it never hurts you. You can get to the point where you can say, "I'll never be hurt another day in my life." Doesn't that sound liberating? We can literally be emotionally invincible. That's what God means when He says that nothing shall by any means hurt us. We can become invincible people. We can become people that are impenetrable. We can become people that cannot be defeated, because real destruction in our lives is not going to come from the outside. It's going to come from within; as is our success.

Our real success is not going to come because somebody gave us a break. Our real success is going to come because we made the right decisions on the inside. It's a series of right decisions—not just one decision; but a series of right decisions that leads us in the right direction.

How can we get to the point where we are never hurt again? How can we become invincible?

Well, there's a right way and a wrong way. Let's look at the wrong way first, so you know what not to do.

THE WRONG WAY TO HANDLE HURT

Chapter Two

1. Our natural response to avoid being hurt is to do the hurting first. "I'm going to attack first." This is some people's way of dealing with hurt. They get on the offensive and they do the hurting first. That's the world's solution. That's not God's solution. Here's the problem with taking the first punch: You are going to reap what you sow. What ends up happening is, it comes back to you in good measure, pressed down, shaken together, and running over!

2. We harden our heart. "I'm not going to let anybody in. I'm just going to harden my heart." The problem with having a hard heart is that you can't hear from God. You can't have meaningful relationships. You become a prisoner of your own pain. So that is not the solution.

3. We pretend we are really not hurt. How many of us have ever done that? We pretend that everything is O.K. The problem with that, is most of us are not great actors, and we end up wearing our hurt on our sleeves. We chant, "Sticks and stones can break my bones but names can never hurt me," but it's just not true. Names do hurt. Words do hurt if you allow them to.

When you pretend that you are not hurt, it puts you out of touch with reality. It invites more mistreatment because you appear to be unmoved by it and unaffected by it. So when you appear to be unaffected by it, the person will keep doing it.

The perfect example of this is in a marriage relationship. If a wife has been hurt by something her husband said or did, she acts as if it didn't bother her. She's going to be tough. The problem with that is that if a man thinks he can get away with something, or that it doesn't bother her, then he may continue to do it. He doesn't know that it affected her in the way that it did because she is communicating, through her actions and through her behavior, that it really didn't hurt her at all. This invites more mistreatment, and more insensitivity on the part of the husband.

4. We decide not to trust anymore. I'm just not going to believe anything that anybody says." The problem with this is it leads to a very lonely and pessimistic life. When you refuse to trust again, it causes you to become cynical and suspicious of everyone that is ever involved in your life—even those that could do you good.

It's important that I clarify at this point, that I'm not saying to put all of your trust in people. I'm simply saying, that to close your heart off and say "I'm just never going to trust anybody ever again" only cuts you off from the blessing that God will bring through godly friends and godly advice—a vital mistake that you don't want to make.

These are some wrong responses to being hurt. However, when you deal with hurt properly, something supernatural happens. People will mistreat you at times. People will wrong you at times. But, 1 Peter 2:19 says, *"For this finds favor, if for the sake of conscience toward God, a person bears up under sorrows when suffering unjustly"* (NASB).

Handle it, put up with it. Have a good attitude and FAVOR will come! God will open doors that no man can close—that's favor.

Simple Steps
To Freedom

≈

Chapter Three

Let me give you this simple process:

1. Take up the shield of faith. This is
so vital, so allow me to take some time to
explain this.

Ephesians 6:16 says that the shield
of faith quenches all the fiery darts of
the enemy.

Faith, simply put, is to believe what God said. When I read my Bible, I am finding out what God said about me. By saying what God says, I am keeping up my shield; and therefore, I won't be hurt. When the fiery dart of sickness comes against me, I can say, "I'm healed by the stripes of Jesus" (1 Peter 2:24). That becomes my shield of faith.

When the fiery dart of mistreatment comes against me, I can say, "No weapon formed against me can prosper" (Isaiah 54:17).

When the fiery dart of financial trouble comes against me, I can say, "My God shall supply all my needs according to His riches and glory" (Philippians 4:19).

Do you see how faith becomes your shield, quenching all the fiery darts of the enemy? But here's the thing you need to understand about this shield of faith: *If the shield is "what God says about us," then when we listen to what other people say about us, we are putting our shield of faith down.* When we put more value on other people's opinions, we are putting our shield of faith down.

Stop placing value on others' opinions of you. We must not put ourselves in a position where their opinions have become more important to us than what God says. Because as soon as we make what they said more important than what God says, we have lowered our shield of faith. As a result, whatever they tell us, becomes our shield. And what they told us isn't enough to protect us.

Now this is true with good things people say and bad things as well. If somebody says something good about you, and you get your sense of self esteem or worth from it, then all that has to happen, to disappoint you, is for them to change their mind.

Ladies, here is an example. If a man says to you, "I really care about you. I really love you," there is sometimes an ulterior motive behind those words. What he may be saying is, "I want you"—not, "I love you." This is how you can know he loves you:

when he doesn't touch you until the day you're married. And when he gives you a ring and says, "My love is backed up with a commitment."

Otherwise this situation can lead to hurt. The man says to a woman, "I love you." And then a few weeks later, he comes back and says, "Well, I don't know how to say this but, um, I've got to break it off."

Now that woman is devastated. Why? Because she put her trust in what he said, rather than in what God said. Do you see how we can be hurt? We set ourselves up for hurt by looking for somebody else to make us happy.

Only Jesus can make us happy. He's the only one that can really make us free.

Don't get me wrong. There's nothing wrong with finding love. There's nothing wrong with marriage. I'm married. And I believe in it! But when I'm trying to get my joy and sense of worth, and sense of confidence from my wife... or when she's trying to get that from me, something's not right.

Why? Because we are setting ourselves up for hurt. If we don't measure up to what the other has expected, then we are going to be sorely disappointed. That's why my wife didn't marry me to get something from me. A person cannot meet your needs! Only God can.

Try this in a relationship: "I trust you, but I don't trust *in* you. I believe you are going to do what you said, but if you don't, I'm not going to lose sleep over it."

Why? Because then, you're not building your life on their promises. You're building your life on God's promises.

2. _If you have been hurt by someone, forgive them as an act of faith._ Don't wait for what I call "inspirational forgiveness." You don't forgive them because you feel like it. You forgive them because you've made a decision to forgive. Forgiveness is a decision, it's not a feeling. The feelings will come later. But if they never come, don't sweat it.

You've made a decision. You've decided, "I forgive this person in Jesus name, and I'm not going to bring it up again." That's a decision you're going to have to make. It's not a feeling. If you wait for the feelings to come, you'll never forgive. So you need to make the decision to forgive. If anybody has hurt you, forgive them.

Sometimes we have thought, "If they just apologize or give me an explanation, then I'll forgive them." Don't hold your breath! It will only make you turn colors. We have also said, "If they change, then I'll forgive them."

Wait a minute—if you can only forgive them when they have changed, then you didn't "for-give." You "for-sold." You "sold" your forgiveness to them. You didn't "give" it to them. There's a difference between giving and selling. Giving means you don't have to pay anything for me to forgive you. Selling means, if you change, then you can buy my forgiveness. No, it's not for sale. It's free.

God didn't forgive you when you changed. You changed *after* He forgave you. So forgive whoever has hurt you and don't ask for an explanation. Don't even ask for an apology. If you need something from them, this reveals your hurt, and your dependence on how they act. You don't need anybody to treat you a certain way in order to feel better.

You need to forgive by faith, and not put so much stock in your feelings. Feelings are more up and down than the stock market.

They are unreliable, and will betray you whenever they *feel* like it.

Forgiveness must be an act of your will. Make the decision and don't look back. This will make you more free than if the person came crawling to you on their hands and knees, begging you for forgiveness. The fact is, if you need them to do that, you really will never be free. It's when what they do doesn't matter anymore, (because your freedom comes from within) that you will be free.

3. Once you forgive, stop re-living it. It reminds me of a story I heard about a little boy that had just scraped his knee, and he had a bandage over it. As you know, when the scab forms, it attaches itself to the bandage. Now, this boy was so excited to show off his scab, that whenever friends came over, he would rip the bandage off, preventing the scab from fully healing. In his desire to let others know what happened to him, he delayed the process of healing.

This is how we often act as Christians. We pull our bandages off all the time and we want somebody to know about how we got hurt. We want somebody to know about what so-and-so did to us or said about us. And every time we talk about it, we are pulling that bandage off. We are delaying the healing process because we continually expose our wound and talk about our pain.

Do you want to never be hurt again? Once you have forgiven someone, stop re-living it.

4. Stop making excuses why you're so easily hurt. "Well I'm a woman, I'm more sensitive." "Well, I'm Italian." "I'm Irish," "I'm black," "I'm Hispanic," "I'm white." We all have a reason to feel we are more sensitive or easily hurt. No! That has nothing to do with it. That's just an excuse.

We are more sensitive, because we're more concerned about our past than our future. We like to talk about our past and revisit our pain. Listen, we have authority over our past and here's what we do with that authority. As Paul the apostle said, *"Forgetting those things that are behind us"* (Philippians 3:13).

Forgetting. Forgetting. Forgetting. Your future is not going to be any different than your past, until you forget about it. You've got to put it behind you. Put behind you what people have done to you. Make your decisions based on God's Word and God's wisdom and not anything that anybody has done to you.

5. Stop wearing your emotions on your sleeve. That's what makes the devil want to pick on you all the time. Remember Rocky? Remember when he went in to the butcher shop and was pounding that side of beef. He kept hitting it in the same spot until he broke the ribs of that cow. When he was fighting Apollo Creed, he kept giving him body blows until he broke his ribs. When he broke one of his ribs, he knew he had wounded him and he kept going after that part of his body.

When the devil knows something hurts you, he's going to keep going after that area of your life.

What do you need to do when the devil has taken his best shot at you? You need to laugh!

Have you ever been in a close call? A near accident of some sort? And you said, "I can't believe that almost happened to me!" You need to respond by praising God! Let the devil know, "You just had your best chance at me and you missed again. And you'll never have a better chance, Mr. devil!"

Oh that frustrates his strategy, when he realizes he's taken his best shot at you and failed! You have to laugh it off. You've got to rejoice. Count it all joy when you encounter various trials.

6. Stop trying to get even with people who have hurt you. The Lord says in Romans 12:19, "*I will have vengeance. I will repay.*" Don't try to play God in the situation and pay back people for what they've done. You let God take care of that. Matthew 5:44 says to pray for those who hurt you.

If somebody has hurt you, bless them. Here's a suggestion: write a list of all the people who have hurt you, and send them all a check. Send them all a gift. Bless them. You say, "Oh man, I'll send them something, all right. I'll send them a dead mouse in a mousetrap!" No—send them a blessing.

The Bible says, do not return evil for evil. But return evil with good. (1 Peter 3:9; I Thessalonians 5:15; Romans 12:21). Do good when somebody mistreats you. We've all been mistreated. We've all been hurt. We've all been talked "nasty" about. We've all been told that we're not going to make it. We've all been lied about. We've all been cheated in some way. We've all been mistreated. But it's over. You're new and it's a new day. Remember, handle it this way, and favor will come.

7. *Take communion over it.* Take communion with the Lord. Take that bread and that cup, and say, "Jesus, based on Your body and Your blood, I release this person. And I'll never hold anything against them again as long as I live." That's powerful stuff.

That cup is the blood of Jesus. It's the blood that forgave you. It's the blood that delivered you. It's the blood that heals you from every weapon formed against you, including hurt!

Because of the blood of Jesus, the Bible says, *"No evil shall befall you"* (Psalm 91:10). Because of the blood of Jesus, the Bible says, *"No weapon formed against you shall prosper"* (Isaiah 54:17).

Conclusion

In conclusion, Jesus said in Luke 10:19,
*"Behold I have given you authority to trample
upon serpents and scorpions and over all the
power of the enemy. **And nothing shall by
any means hurt you!"***

As you follow these steps, you are walking
in your God-given authority. You are putting
your trust in God. And He will never let you
down. Numbers 23:19 says, *"He is not a man
that He should lie."* Whatever He has promised

you, He will be faithful to do it. Though others may let you down, He will never leave you or forsake you!

Meditate on His love for you. Romans 5:5 says, *"The love of God has been shed abroad in your heart... therefore, you can have hope... and hope never disappoints."*

Now abide these three—faith, hope and love—and you will never be hurt again!

ABOUT THE AUTHOR

Gregory Dickow is the host of "Changing Your Life," a dynamic television show seen throughout the world, reaching a potential half a billion households. He is also the founder and Senior Pastor of Life Changers International Church, a diverse and thriving congregation in the Chicago area with several thousand in weekly attendance.

Known for his ability to communicate the power and principles of God's Word clearly and concisely, Pastor Dickow lives to see the lives of people dramatically changed forever.

Pastor Dickow is also the host of "Ask the Pastor" a live radio show reaching the world through radio and the internet with live callers asking hard-hitting questions about their real-life problems. Pastor Dickow is reaching people personally, encouraging them and empowering them to succeed in every area of life.

Other Books Available by Pastor Gregory Dickow

- Acquiring Beauty
- Breaking the Power of Inferiority
- Conquering Your Flesh
- Financial Freedom
- How to Hear the Voice of God
- How to Never Be Hurt Again
- Taking Charge of Your Emotions
- The Power to Change Anything
- Winning the Battle of the Mind

Audio Series available by Pastor Gregory Dickow

- Financial Freedom: Strategies for a Blessed Life
- How to Pray & Get Results
- Love Thyself
- Mastering Your Emotions
- Redeemed from the Curse
- The Blood Covenant
- Building Your Marriage God's Way

You can order these and many other life-changing materials by calling toll-free 1-888-438-5433.

For more information about Gregory Dickow Ministries and a free product catalog, please visit www.changinglives.org